The Advent Keepsake.

Advent Keepsake

Compiled by a Believer

© 2018 Waymark Books.

All rights reserved. No part of this publication may be reproduced, stored in a retrieval system or transmited in any form or by any means, electronic, mechanical, photocopying, recording or otherwise without the prior permision of the publisher or in accordance with the provisions of the Copyright, Designs and Patents Act 1988 or under the terms of any licence permitting limited copying issued by the Copyright Licensing Agency.

Published by:
Waymark Books
PO Box 7
Cedar Lake, MI 48812 USA

ISBN-13: 978-1611046908

THE
Advent Keepsake
— OR —
A Text for Each Day of the Year

ON THE SUBJECTS
OF CHRIST'S SECOND COMING — THE RESURRECTION
THE NEW EARTH — PROMISES FOR
THE TIME OF TROUBLE, ETC.

COMPILED BY A BELIEVER.

STEAM PRESS
of the Seventh-day Adventist Publishing Association
BATTLE CREEK, MICHIGAN
1868.

TO THE
Household of Faith,
WHO ARE LOOKING FOR
THAT BLESSED HOPE,
The Appearing of our Savior,
THIS LITTLE KEEPSAKE
Is affectionately
DEDICATED.

BEHOLD, I COME QUICKLY.

TO THE READER

THIS little Keepsake has been prepared solely for the purpose of ministering consolation to the children of God, who, in the midst of great trials and temptations, are awaiting the fulfillment of the promises. In no way could this so effectually be done as in the very words of the Scriptures. Having this object continually in mind, the Compiler has aimed to select only those texts which are of a consolatory character. Of course, this work is no attempt at literary skill.

The arrangement is such that the thoughtful reader will get from it a pretty clear idea of the teachings of the Scriptures on the Second Coming of Christ. Our little volume, then, is purely adventical, both in letter and in spirit. In it are presented most of those comforting portions which speak of the final deliverance of the people of God. What could be more appropriate for the church now in this time of patient waiting for Christ! May it be to them as Jacob's gift to Pharoah, "a little balm, and a little honey, spices and myrrh, nuts and almonds." (Genesis 43:11.)

If by reading this Keepsake, and meditating upon its contents, the attention of any shall be more fully directed to the contemplation of that greatest of all events, the glorious appearing of our Lord Jesus Christ, the highest expectations of the compiler will be fully realized. May the blessing of HIM who will soon be seen "on the white cloud," go with it.

***

THE
𝔄𝔡𝔳𝔢𝔫𝔱 𝔎𝔢𝔢𝔭𝔰𝔞𝔨𝔢

JANUARY.

1. Unto them that look for Him, shall He appear the second time without sin unto salvation. HEBREWS 9:28

2. Wherefore we receiving a kingdom which cannot be moved, let us have grace, whereby we may serve God acceptably, with reverence and godly fear. HEBREWS 12:28

3. Be patient therefore, brethren, unto the coming of the Lord. Behold, the husbandman waiteth for the precious fruit of the earth, and hath long patience for it, until he receive the early and latter rain. JAMES 5:7

4. Beloved, think it not strange concerning the fiery trial which is to try you, as though some strange thing happened unto you: but rejoice, inasmuch as ye are partakers of Christ's sufferings; that, when his glory shall be revealed, ye may be glad also with exceeding joy. 1 PETER 4:12-13

ADVENT KEEPSAKE.

5. Be ye therefore sober, and watch unto prayer. 1 PETER 4:7

6. And when the chief Shepherd shall appear, ye shall receive a crown of glory that fadeth not away. 1 PETER 5:4

7. Behold, he cometh with clouds; and every eye shall see him, and they also which pierced him: and all kindreds of the earth shall wail because of him. Even so, Amen. REVELATION 1:7

8. To him that overcometh will I give to eat of the tree of life, which is in the midst of the paradise of God. REVELATION 2:7

9. Behold, the Lord cometh with ten thousands of his saints. JUDE 14

10. Then shall we know, if we follow on to know the Lord: his going forth is prepared as the morning; and he shall come unto us as the rain, as the latter and former rain unto the earth. HOSEA 6:3

11. He that overcometh shall not be hurt of the second death. REVELATION. 2:11

JANUARY.

12. Behold, I come quickly: hold that fast which thou hast, that no man take thy crown. REVELATION 3:11

13. Seek ye the Lord, all ye meek of the earth, which have wrought his judgment; seek righteousness, seek meekness: it may be ye shall be hid in the day of the Lord's anger. ZEPHANIAH 2:3

14. And the kingdom and dominion, and the greatness of the kingdom under the whole heaven, shall be given to the people of the saints of the Most High. DANIEL 7:27

15. Gather yourselves together, yea, gather together, O nation not desired; before the decree bring forth, before the day pass as the chaff, before the fierce anger of the Lord come upon you, before the day of the Lord's anger come upon you. ZEPHANIAH 2:1-2

16. Let not your heart be troubled: ye believe in God, believe also in me. JOHN 14:1

17. This same Jesus, which is taken up from you into Heaven, shall so come in like manner as ye have seen him go into Heaven. ACTS 1:11

ADVENT KEEPSAKE.

18. I will also leave in the midst of thee an afflicted and poor people, and they shall trust in the name of the Lord. ZEPHANIAH 3:12

19. And the Lord direct your hearts into the love of God, and into the patient waiting for Christ. 2 THESSALONIANS 3:5

20. To him that overcometh will I give to eat of the hidden manna, and will give him a white stone, and in the stone a new name written, which no man knoweth saving he that receiveth it. REVELATION 2:17

21. The remnant of Israel shall not do iniquity, nor speak lies; neither shall a deceitful tongue be found in their mouth. ZEPHANIAH 3:13

22. Because thou hast kept the word of my patience, I also will keep thee from the hour of temptation, which shall come upon all the world, to try them that dwell upon the earth. REVELATION 3:10

23. And I looked, and, lo, a Lamb stood on the Mount Sion, and with him a hundred forty and four thousand, having his Father's name written in their foreheads. REVELATION 14:1

JANUARY.

24. Let the heavens rejoice, and let the earth be glad; let the sea roar, and the fulness thereof. Let the field be joyful, and all that is therein: then shall all the trees of the wood rejoice before the Lord: for he cometh, for he cometh to judge the earth: he shall judge the world with righteousness, and the people with his truth. PSALM 96:11-13

25. Because thou hast made the Lord, which is my refuge, even the Most High, thy habitation; there shall no evil befall thee, neither shall any plague come nigh thy dwelling. PSALM 91:9-10

26. Beloved, now are we the sons of God, and it doth not yet appear what we shall be: but we know that, when he shall appear, we shall be like him; for we shall see him as he is. 1 JOHN 3:2

27. But the day of the Lord will come as a thief in the night; in the which the heavens shall pass away with a great noise, and the elements shall melt with fervent heat, the earth also and the works that are therein shall be burned up. 2 PETER 3:10

ADVENT KEEPSAKE.

28. And every man that hath this hope in him purifieth himself, even as he is pure. 1 JOHN 3:3

29. And now, little children, abide in him; that, when he shall appear, we may have confidence, and not be ashamed before him at his coming. 1 JOHN 2:28

30. Let us hear the conclusion of the whole matter: Fear God, and keep his commandments: for this is the whole duty of man. For God shall bring every work into judgment, with every secret thing, whether it be good, or whether it be evil. ECCLESIASTES 12:13-14

31. Now unto Him that is able to keep you from falling, and to present you faultless before the presence of his glory with exceeding joy, to the only wise God our Saviour, be glory and majesty, dominion and power, both now and ever. JUDE 24-25

FEBRUARY.

1. Fear not, little flock; for it is your Father's good pleasure to give you the kingdom. LUKE 12:32

2. Oh, how great is thy goodness, which thou hast laid up for them that fear thee; which thou hast wrought for them that trust in thee before the sons of men! PSALM 31:19

3. The Lord is known by the judgment which he executeth. PSALM 9:16

4. For the day of the Lord of hosts shall be upon every one that is proud and lofty, and upon every one that is lifted up; and he shall be brought low: and upon all the cedars of Lebanon, that are high and lifted up, and upon all the oaks of Bashan, and upon all the high mountains, and upon all the hills that are lifted up, and upon every high tower, and upon every fenced wall, and upon all the ships of Tarshish, and upon all pleasant pictures. And the loftiness of man shall be bowed down, and the haughtiness of men shall be made low; and the Lord alone shall be exalted in that day. ISAIAH 2:12-17

ADVENT KEEPSAKE.

5. And he that sat upon the throne said, Behold, I make all things new. REVELATION 21:5

6. And Enoch walked with God: and he was not; for God took him. GENESIS 5:24

7. The scepter shall not depart from Judah, nor a lawgiver from between his feet, until Shiloh come; and unto him shall the gathering of the people be. GENESIS 49:10

8. So man lieth down, and riseth not; till the heavens be no more, they shall not awake, nor be raised out of their sleep. JOB 14:12

9. Blessed is the man that walketh not in the counsel of the ungodly, nor standeth in the way of sinners, nor sitteth in the seat of the scornful. But his delight is in the law of the Lord; and in his law doth he meditate day and night. And he shall be like a tree planted by the rivers of water, that bringeth forth his fruit in his season; his leaf also shall not wither, and whatsoever he doeth shall prosper. PSALM 1:1-3

10. Ask of me, and I shall give thee the heathen for thine inheritance, and the uttermost parts of the earth for thy possession. PSALM 2:8

FEBRUARY.

11. Behold, I come quickly: blessed is he that keepeth the sayings of the prophecy of this book. REVELATION 22:7

12. And the Spirit and the bride say, Come. And let him that heareth say, Come. And let him that is athirst come. And whosoever will, let him take the water of life freely. REVELATION 22:17

13. Zion shall be redeemed with judgment, and her converts with righteousness. ISAIAH 1:27

14. Enter into the rock, and hide thee in the dust, for fear of the Lord, and for the glory of his majesty. The lofty looks of man shall be humbled, and the haughtiness of men shall be bowed down; and the Lord alone shall be exalted in that day. ISAIAH 2:10-11

15. For the Son of man shall come in the glory of his Father with his angels; and then he shall reward every man according to his works. MATTHEW 16:27

16. But who may abide the day of his coming? and who shall stand when he appeareth? for he is like a refiner's fire, and like fuller's soap. MALACHI 3:2

ADVENT KEEPSAKE.

17. Then they that feared the Lord spake often one to another: and the Lord hearkened, and heard it, and a book of remembrance was written before him for them that feared the Lord, and that thought upon his name. MALACHI 3:16

18. But the meek shall inherit the earth; and shall delight themselves in the abundance of peace. PSALM 37:11

19. And I looked, and behold a white cloud, and upon the cloud one sat like unto the Son of man, having on his head a golden crown, and in his hand a sharp sickle. REVELATION 14:14

20. Thy throne, O God, is for ever and ever: the scepter of thy kingdom is a right scepter. PSALM 14:6

21. The King's daughter is all glorious within: her clothing is of wrought gold. She shall be brought unto the King in raiment of needlework: the virgins her companions that follow her shall be brought unto thee. With gladness and rejoicing shall they be brought: they shall enter into the King's palace. PSALM 45:13-15

22. Oh, that the salvation of Israel were come out of Zion! When God bringeth back the captivity

FEBRUARY.

of his people, Jacob shall rejoice, and Israel shall be glad. PSALM 53:6

23. O clap your hands all ye people; shout unto God with the voice of triumph. For the Lord most high is terrible; he is a great King over all the earth. He shall subdue the people under us, and the nations under our feet. He shall choose our inheritance for us, the excellency of Jacob whom he loved. Selah. PSALM 47:1-4

24. Our God shall come, and shall not keep silence: a fire shall devour before him, and it shall be very tempestuous round about him. He shall call to the heavens from above, and to the earth, that he may judge his people. PSALM 50:3

25. Gather my saints together unto me; those that have made a covenant with me by sacrifice. And the heavens shall declare his righteousness: for God is judge himself. Selah. PSALM 50:5-6

26. How hardly shall they that have riches enter into the kingdom of God! LUKE 28:24

27. And he shewed me a pure river of water of life, clear as crystal, proceeding out of the throne of God and of the Lamb. REVELATION 22:1

ADVENT KEEPSAKE.

28. And God shall wipe away all tears from their eyes; and there shall be no more death, neither sorrow, nor crying, neither shall there be any more pain: for the former things are passed away. REVELATION 21:4

29. He that overcometh shall inherit all things: and I will be his God, and he shall be my son. REVELATION 21:7

MARCH.

1. Behold, a King shall reign in righteousness, and princes shall rule in judgment. ISAIAH 32:1

2. Nevertheless we, according to his promise, look for new heavens and a new earth, wherein dwelleth righteousness. 2 PETER 3:13

3. But there the glorious Lord will be unto us a place of broad rivers and streams; wherein shall go no galley with oars, neither shall gallant ship pass thereby. ISAIAH 33:21

4. And the ransomed of the Lord shall return, and come to Zion with songs and everlasting joy upon their heads: they shall obtain joy and gladness, and sorrow and sighing shall flee away. ISAIAH 35:10

5. And I heard a great voice out of heaven saying, Behold, the tabernacle of God is with men, and he will dwell with them, and they shall be his people, and God himself shall be with them, and be their God. REVELATION 21:3

ADVENT KEEPSAKE.

6. Come, behold the works of the Lord, what desolations he hath made in the earth. He maketh wars to cease unto the end of the earth; he breaketh the bow, and cutteth the spear in sunder; he burneth the chariot in the fire. Be still, and know that I am God: I will be exalted among the heathen, I will be exalted in the earth. PSALM 46:8-10

7. For we must needs die, and are as water spilt on the ground, which cannot be gathered up again; neither doth God respect any person; yet doth he devise means, that his banished be not expelled from him. 2 SAMUEL 14:14

8. Say to them that are of a fearful heart, Be strong, fear not: behold, your God will come with vengeance, even God with a recompense; he will come and save you. ISAIAH 35:4

9. Verily I say unto you, There be some standing here, which shall not taste of death till they see the Son of man coming in his kingdom. MATTHEW 16:28

10. Can ye not discern the signs of the times? MATTHEW 16:3

MARCH.

11. Arise, O Lord, in thine anger, lift up thyself because of the rage of mine enemies: and awake for me to the judgment that thou hast commanded. PSALM 7:6

12. Oh! let the wickedness of the wicked come to an end; but establish the just: for the righteous God trieth the hearts and reins. PSALM 7:9

13. By grace ye are saved. EPHESIANS 2:5

14. This know also, that in the last days perilous times shall come. 2 TIMOTHY 3:1

15. But he that shall endure unto the end, the same shall be saved. MATTHEW 24:13

16. And call upon me in the day of trouble: I will deliver thee, and thou shalt glorify me. PSALM 50:15

17. And this gospel of the kingdom shall be preached in all the world for a witness unto all nations; and then shall the end come. MATTHEW 24:14

18. Oh, that the salvation of Israel were come out of Zion! when the Lord bringeth back the captivity of his people, Jacob shall rejoice, and Israel shall be glad. PSALM 14:7

ADVENT KEEPSAKE.

19. As for me, I will behold thy face in righteousness: I shall be satisfied when I awake, with thy likeness. PSALM 17:15

20. The Lord hear thee in the day of trouble; the name of the God of Jacob defend thee; send thee help from the sanctuary, and strengthen thee out of Zion. PSALM 20:1-2

21. When Christ, who is our life, shall appear, then shall ye also appear with him in glory. COLOSSIANS 3:4

22. But the Lord shall endure for ever: he hath prepared his throne for judgment. And he shall judge the world in righteousness, he shall minister judgment to the people in uprightness. PSALM 9:7-8

23. Who shall ascend into the hill of the Lord? or who shall stand in his holy place? He that hath clean hands and a pure heart; who hath not lifted up his soul unto vanity, nor sworn deceitfully. He shall receive the blessing from the Lord, and righteousness from the God of his salvation. PSALM 24:3-5

24. For in the time of trouble he shall hide me in his pavilion: in the secret of his tabernacle

MARCH.

shall he hide me; he shall set me up upon a rock. PSALM 27:5

25. And they shall go into the holes of the rocks, and into the caves of the earth, for fear of the Lord, and for the glory of his majesty, when he ariseth to shake terribly the earth. ISAIAH 2:19

26. In that day a man shall cast his idols of silver, and his idols of gold, which they made each one for himself to worship, to the moles and to the bats; to go into the clefts of the rocks, and into the tops of the ragged rocks, for fear of the Lord, and for the glory of his majesty, when he ariseth to shake terribly the earth. Cease ye from man, whose breath is in his nostrils: for wherein is he to be accounted of? ISAIAH 2:20-22

27. Seeing then that all these things shall be dissolved, what manner of persons ought ye to be in all holy conversation and godliness, looking for and hasting unto the coming of the day of God, wherein the heavens being on fire shall be dissolved, and the elements shall melt with fervent heat? 2 PETER 3:11-12

28. Wherefore, beloved, seeing that ye look for such things, be diligent that ye may be found

ADVENT KEEPSAKE.

of him in peace, without spot, and blameless. 2 PETER 3:14

29. He that overcometh, the same shall be clothed in white raiment; and I will not blot out his name out of the book of life, but I will confess his name before my Father, and before his angels. REVELATION 3:5

30. He that hath an ear, let him hear what the Spirit saith unto the churches. REVELATION 3:22

31. Blessed are those servants, whom the Lord when he cometh shall find watching: verily I say unto you, that he shall gird himself, and make them to sit down to meat, and will come forth and serve them. LUKE 12:37

APRIL.

1. Send out thy light and thy truth; let them lead me; let them bring me unto thy holy hill, and to thy tabernacles. PSALM 43:3

2. Be ye therefore ready also: for the Son of man cometh at an hour when ye think not. LUKE 12:40

3. Blessed are they that do his commandments, that they may have right to the tree of life, and may enter in through the gates into the city. REVELATION 22:14

4. Herein is our love made perfect, that we may have boldness in the day of judgment: because as he is, so are we in this world. 1 JOHN 4:17

5. The righteous shall rejoice when he seeth the vengeance: he shall wash his feet in the blood of the wicked. So that a man shall say, Verily there is a reward for the righteous: verily he is a God that judgeth in the earth. PSALM 58:10-11

ADVENT KEEPSAKE.

6. O let the nations be glad and sing for joy: for thou shalt judge the people righteously, and govern the nations upon earth. PSALM 67:4

7. Blessed is he that shall eat bread in the kingdom of God. LUKE 14:15

8. For his anger endureth but a moment; in his favor is life; weeping may endure for a night, but joy cometh in the morning. PSALM 30:5

9. Immediately after the tribulation of those days shall the sun be darkened, and the moon shall not give her light, and the stars shall fall from heaven, and the powers of the heavens shall be shaken. And then shall appear the sign of the Son of man in heaven: and then shall all the tribes of the earth mourn, and they shall see the Son of man coming in the clouds of heaven with power and great glory. MATTHEW 24:29-30

10. And he shall send his angels with a great sound of a trumpet, and they shall gather together his elect from the four winds, from one end of heaven to the other. MATTHEW 24:31

11. Now learn a parable of the fig tree; when his branch is yet tender, and putteth forth leaves,

APRIL.

ye know that summer is nigh: so likewise ye, when ye shall see all these things, know that it is near, even at the doors. MATTHEW 24: 32-33

12. Holding forth the word of life; that I may rejoice in the day of Christ, that I have not run in vain, neither labored in vain. PHILIPPIANS 2:16

13. But when thou makest a feast, call the poor, the maimed, the lame, the blind: and thou shalt be blessed; for they cannot recompense thee; for thou shalt be recompensed at the resurrection of the just. LUKE 14:13-14

14. For as the lightning cometh out of the east, and shineth even unto the west; so shall also the coming of the Son of man be. MATTHEW 24:27

15. O God, thou art terrible out of thy holy places: the God of Israel is he that giveth strength and power unto his people. Blessed be God. PSALM 68:38

16. Thou, which hast shewed me great and sore troubles, shalt quicken me again, and shalt bring me up again from the depths of the

ADVENT KEEPSAKE.

earth. Thou shalt increase my greatness, and comfort me on every side. PSALM 71:21

17. Give the king thy judgments, O God, and thy righteousness unto the king's son. In his days shall the righteous flourish; and abundance of peace so long as the moon endureth. He shall have dominion also from sea to sea, and from the river unto the ends of the earth. PSALM 72:1,7,8

18. And, behold, I come quickly; and my reward is with me, to give every man according as his work shall be. REVELATION 22:12

19. I press toward the mark for the prize of the high calling of God in Christ Jesus. PHILIPPIANS 3:14

20. Knowing that of the Lord ye shall receive the reward of the inheritance. COLOSSIANS 3:23

21. For evil doers shall be cut off; but those that wait upon the Lord, they shall inherit the earth. PSALM 37:9

22. The Lord knoweth the davs of the upright; and their inheritance shall be for ever. They shall not be ashamed in the evil time; and in the days of famine they shall be satisfied. PSALM 37:18-19

APRIL.

23. For the Son of man is as a man taking a far journey, who left his house, and gave authority to his servants, and to every man his work, and commanded the porter to watch. Watch ye therefore; for ye know not when the master of the house cometh, at even, or at midnight, or at the cock-crowing, or in the morning. MARK 13:34-35

24. Let your loins be girded about, and your lights burning; and ye yourselves like unto men that wait for their Lord, when he will return from the wedding; that when he cometh and knocketh, they may open unto him immediately. LUKE 12:35-36

25. In whom ye also trusted, after that ye heard the word of truth, the gospel of your salvation: in whom also, after that ye believed, ye were sealed with that Holy Spirit of promise, which is the earnest of our inheritance until the redemption of the purchased possession, unto the praise of His glory. EPHESIANS 2:13-14

26. Now unto him that is able to do exceeding abundantly above all that we ask or think, according to the power that worketh in us, unto him be glory in the church by Christ

ADVENT KEEPSAKE.

Jesus throughout all ages, world without end. Amen. EPHESIANS 3:20-21

27. And the very God of peace sanctify you wholly; and I pray God your whole spirit and soul and body be preserved blameless unto the coming of our Lord Jesus Christ. 1 THESSALONIANS 5:23

28. For God hath not appointed us to wrath, but to obtain salvation by our Lord Jesus Christ. 1 THESSALONIANS 5:9

29. Now the Spirit speaketh expressly that in the latter times some shall depart from the faith. 1 TIMOTHY 4:1

30. And therefore will the Lord wait, that he may be gracious unto you, and therefore will he be exalted, that he may have mercy upon you: for the Lord is a God of judgment: blessed are all they that wait for him. ISAIAH 30:18

MAY.

1. Blessed be the Lord God, the God of Israel, who only doeth wondrous things. And blessed be his glorious name forever and let the whole earth be filled with his glory. Amen, and Amen. PSALM 72:18-19

2. Thou shalt guide me with thy counsel, and afterward receive me to glory. PSALM 73:24

3. And I John saw the holy city, new Jerusalem, coming down from God out of Heaven, prepared as a bride adorned for, her husband. REVELATION 21:2

4. Wait on the Lord, and keep his way, and he shall exalt thee to inherit the land: when the wicked are cut off, thou shalt see it. PSALM 37:34

5. For in the hand of the Lord there is a cup, and the wine is red; it is full of mixture; and he poureth out of the same: but the dregs thereof, all the wicked of the earth shall wring them out, and drink them. But I will declare for

ADVENT KEEPSAKE.

ever; I will sing praises to the God of Jacob. PSALM 75:8-9

6. And when these things begin to come to pass, then look up, and lift up your heads; for your redemption draweth nigh. LUKE 21:28

7. Thou didst cause judgment to be heard from Heaven; the earth feared, and was still, when God arose to judgment, to save all the meek of the earth. Selah. Surely the wrath of man shall praise thee: the remainder of wrath shalt thou restrain. PSALM 76:8-10

8. Watch ye therefore, and pray always, that ye may be accounted worthy to escape all these things that shall come to pass, and to stand before the Son of man. LUKE 21:36

9. For such as be blessed of him shall inherit the earth. PSALM 37:22

10. And shall not God avenge his own elect, which cry day and night unto him, though he bear long with them? LUKE 18:7

11. All nations whom thou hast made shall come and worship before thee, O Lord; and shall glorify thy name. For thou art great, and doest

MAY.

wondrous things: thou art God alone. PSALM 86:9-10

12. And of Zion it shall be said, This and that man was born in her: and the Highest himself shall establish her. The Lord shall count, when he writeth up the people, that this man was born there. Selah. PSALM 87:5-6

13. And I saw a great white throne, and Him that sat on it, from whose face the earth and the heaven fled away; and there was found no place for them. REVELATION 20:11

14. Then shall the King say unto them on his right hand, Come, ye blessed of my Father, inherit the kingdom prepared for you from the foundation of the world. MATTHEW 25:34

15. Thou shalt arise, and have mercy upon Zion; for the time to favor her, yea, the set time is come. When the Lord shall build up Zion, he shall appear in his glory. Ps. cii, 13, 16.

16. Bless the Lord, 0 my soul, and (forget not all his benefits : who forgiveth all thine iniquities; who healeth all thy diseases. Ps. ciii, 2, 3.

17. But the mercy of the Lord is from everlasting to everlasting upon them that 0 fear him, and

ADVENT KEEPSAKE.

his righteousness unto children's children; to such as keep his covenant, and to those that remember his commandments to do them. Psalm 103:17-18

18. For our conversation is in Heaven; from whence also we look for the Saviour, the Lord Jesus Christ: who shall change our vile body, that it may be fashioned like unto his glorious body, according to the working whereby he is able even to subdue all things unto himself. PHILIPPIANS 3:20-21

19. I charge thee therefore before God, and the Lord Jesus Christ, who shall judge the quick and the dead at his appearing and his kingdom, Preach the word; be instant in season, out of season; reprove, rebuke, exhort with all long-suffering and doctrine. 2 TIMOTHY 4:1-2

20. God is our refuge and strength, a very present help in trouble. Therefore will we not fear, though the earth be removed, and though the mountains be carried into the midst of the sea; though the waters thereof roar and be troubled, though the mountains shake with the swelling thereof. PSALM 46:1-3

MAY.

21. Thy people shall be willing in the day of thy power, in the beauties of holiness from the womb of the morning: thou hast the dew of thy youth. The Lord at thy right hand shall strike through kings in the day of his wrath. PSALM 110:3,5

22. They that trust in the Lord shall be as Mount Zion, which cannot be removed, but abideth forever. As the mountains are round about Jerusalem, so the Lord is round about his people from henceforth even for ever. Psalm 125:1-2

23. And every one that hath forsaken houses, or brethren, or sisters, or father, or mother, or wife, or children, or lands, for my name's sake, shall receive a hundredfold, and shall inherit everlasting life. MATTHEW 19:29

24. But many that are first shall be last; and the last shall be first. MATTHEW 19:30

25. And I appoint unto you a kingdom, as my Father hath appointed unto me; that ye may eat and drink at my table in my kingdom, and sit on thrones judging the twelve tribes of Israel. MATTHEW 22:29-30

ADVENT KEEPSAKE.

26. They that sow in tears shall reap in joy. He that goeth forth and weepeth, bearing precious seed, shall doubtless come again with rejoicing, bringing his sheaves with him. PSALM 126:5-6

27. All thy works shall praise thee, O Lord; and thy saints shall bless thee. They shall speak of the glory of thy kingdom, and talk of thy power; to make known to the sons of men his mighty acts, and the glorious majesty of his kingdom. Thy kingdom is an everlasting kingdom, and thy dominion endureth throughout all generations. PSALM 145:10-13

28. Finally, brethren, whatsoever things are true, whatsoever things are honest, whatsoever things are just, whatsoever things are pure, whatsoever things are lovely, whatsoever things are of good report; if there be any virtue, and if there be any praise, think on these things. PHILIPPIANS 4:8

29. Verily I say unto you, Except ye be converted, and become as little children, ye shall not enter into the kingdom of Heaven. MATTHEW 18:3

30. Whosoever therefore shall humble himself as this little child, the same is greatest in the kingdom of Heaven. MATTHEW 18:4

MAY.

31. Now unto the King eternal, immortal, invisible, the only wise God, be honor and glory for ever and ever. Amen. 1 TIMOTHY 1:17

JUNE.

1. For yet a little while, and He that shall come will come, and will not tarry. HEBREWS 10:37

2. Cast not away therefore your confidence, which hath great recompense of reward. HEBREWS 10:35

3. For, behold, the day cometh that shall burn as an oven; and all the proud, yea, and all that do wickedly, shall be stubble: and the day that cometh shall burn them up, saith the Lord of hosts, that it shall leave them neither root nor branch. But unto you that fear my name shall the Sun of righteousness arise with healing in his wings; and ye shall go forth, and grow up as calves of the stall. MALACHI 4:1-2

4. And ye shall be hated of all men for my name's sake: but he that endureth to the end shall be saved. MATTHEW 10:22

5. The upright shall dwell in the land, and the perfect shall remain in it. PROVERBS 2:21

JUNE.

6. But the path of the just is as the shining light, that shineth more and more unto the perfect day. PROVERBS 4:18

7. If we suffer, we shall also reign with him. 2 TIMOTHY 2:12

8. All Scripture is given by inspiration of God, and is profitable for doctrine, for reproof, for correction, for instruction in righteousness: that the man of God may be perfect, thoroughly furnished unto all good works. 2 TIMOTHY 3:16-17

9. Rejoice, 0 young man, in thy youth; and let thy heart cheer thee in the days of thy youth, and walk in the ways of thine heart, and in the sight of thine eyes: but know thou, that for all these things God will bring thee into judgment. ECCLESIASTES 11:9

10. Brethren, if any of you do err from the truth, and one convert him; let him know, that he which converteth the sinner from the error of his way, shall save a soul from death, and shall hide a multitude of sins. JAMES 5:19-20

11. And I saw a new heaven and a new earth: for the first heaven and the first earth were passed

ADVENT KEEPSAKE.

away; and there was no more sea. REVELATION 21:1

12. Henceforth there is laid up for me a crown of righteousness, which the Lord, the righteous judge, shall give me at that day: and not to me only, but unto all them also that love his appearing. 2 TIMOTHY 4:8

13. Hearken, my beloved brethren, hath not God chosen the poor of this world rich in faith, and heirs of the kingdom which he hath promised to them that love him? JAMES 2:5

14. For here we have no continuing city, but we seek one to come. HEBREWS 13:4

15. I lead in the way of righteousness, in the midst of the paths of judgment: that I may cause those that love me to inherit substance. PROVERBS 8:20-21

16. The righteous shall never be removed: but the wicked shall not inhabit the earth. PROVERBS 10:30

17. Therefore be ye also ready: for in such an hour as ye think not the Son of man cometh. MATTHEW 24:44

JUNE.

18. But ye are come unto Mount Sion, and unto the city of the living God, the heavenly Jerusalem, and to an innumerable company of angels, to the general assembly and church of the firstborn, which are written in Heaven, and to God the Judge of all, and to the spirits of just men made perfect. HEBREWS 12:22-23

19. Comfort ye, comfort ye my people, saith your God. Speak ye comfortably to Jerusalem, and cry unto her, that her warfare is accomplished, that her iniquity is pardoned: for she hath received of the Lord's hand double for all her sins. ISAIAH 40:1

20. Behold, the Lord God will come with strong hand, and his arm shall rule for him: behold, his reward is with him, and his work before him. ISAIAH 40:10

21. One generation passeth away, and another generation cometh: but the earth abideth for ever. ECCLESIASTES 1:4

22. The Lord is good, a strong hold in the day of trouble: and he knoweth them that trust in him. NAHUM 1:7

ADVENT KEEPSAKE.

23. The shield of his mighty men is made red, the valiant men are in scarlet: the chariots shall be with flaming torches in the day of His preparation, and the fir trees shall be terribly shaken. The char- iots shall rage in the streets, they shall justle one against another in the broad ways: they shall seem like torches, they shall run like the lightnings. NAHUM 2:3-4

24. Then said Jesus unto his disciples, If any man will come after me, let him deny himself, and take up his cross, and follow me. MATTHEW 16:24

25. And Jesus said unto them, Verily I say unto you, That ye which have followed me, in the regeneration when the Son of man shall sit in the throne of his glory, ye also shall sit upon twelve thrones, judging the twelve tribes of Israel. MATTHEW 19:28

26. Come unto me, all ye that labor and are heavy laden, and I will give you rest. Take my yoke upon you, and learn of me; for I am meek and lowly in heart: and ye shall find rest unto your souls. For my yoke is easy, and my burden is light. MATTHEW 11:28-30

JUNE.

27. For I reckon that the sufferings of this present time are not worthy to be compared with the glory which shall be revealed in us. For the earnest expectation of the creature waiteth for the mani- festation of the sons of God. ROMANS 8:18-19

28. And to you who are troubled, rest with us, when the Lord Jesus shall be revealed from Heaven with his mighty angels, in flaming fire, taking vengeance on them that know not God, and that obey not the gospel of our Lord Jesus Christ: who shall be punished with everlasting destruction from the presence of the Lord, and from the glory of his power; when he shall come to be glorified in his saints, and to be admired in all them that believe (because our testimony among you was believed) in that day. 2 THESSALONIANS 1:7-10

29. Let the floods clap their hands: let the hills be joyful together before the Lord; for he cometh to judge the earth: with righteousness shall he judge the world, and the people with equity. PSALM 98:8-9

30. Now our Lord Jesus Christ himself, and God, even our Father, which hath loved us, and

ADVENT KEEPSAKE.

hath given us everlasting consolation and good hope through grace, comfort your hearts, and stablish you in every good word and work. 2 THESSALONIANS 2:16-17

JULY.

1. For I know that my Redeemer liveth, and that he shall stand at the latter day upon the earth: and though after my skin worms destroy this body, yet in my flesh shall I see God. JOB 19:25-26

2. God will redeem my soul from the power of the grave; for he shall receive me. Selah. PSALM 49:15

3. Verily, verily, I say unto you, The hour is coming, and now is, when the dead shall hear the voice of the Son of God: and they that hear shall live. JOHN 5:25

4. But sanctify the Lord God in your hearts: and be ready always to give an answer to every man that asketh you a reason of the hope that is in you, with meekness and fear. 1 PETER 3:15

5. Marvel not at this: for the hour is coming, in the which all that are in the graves shall hear his voice, and shall come forth; they that have done good, unto the resurrection of life; and

ADVENT KEEPSAKE.

they that have done evil, unto the resurrection of damnation. JOHN 5:28-29

6. Behold, the Lord hath proclaimed unto the end of the world, Say ye to the daughter of Zion, Behold, thy salvation cometh; behold, his reward is with him, And his work before him. ISAIAH 62:11

7. Who is this that cometh from Edom, with dyed garments from Bozrah? this that is glorious in his apparel, traveling in the greatness of his strength? I that speak in righteousness, mighty to save. Wherefore art thou red in thine apparel, and thy garments like him that treadeth in the winefat? I have trodden the winepress alone; and of the people there was none with me; for I will tread them in mine anger, and trample them in my fury; and their blood shall be sprinkled upon my garments, and I will stain all my raiment. For the day of vengeance is in mine heart, and the year of my redeemed is come. ISAIAH 63:1-4

8. Blessed are the meek; for they shall inherit the earth. MATTHEW 5:5

JULY.

9. And the inhabitant shall not say, I am sick: the people that dwell therein shall be forgiven their iniquity. ISAIAH 33:24

10. Ask ye of the Lord rain in the time of the latter rain; so the Lord shall make bright clouds, and give them showers of rain, to every one grass in the field. ZECHARIAH 10:1

11. But the God of all grace, who hath called us unto his eternal glory by Christ Jesus, after that ye have suffered awhile, make you perfect, stablish, strengthen, settle you. 1 PETER 5:10

12. Thus saith the Lord, Keep ye judgment and do justice: for my salvation is near to come, and my righteousness to be revealed. ISAIAH 56:1

13. Verily, I say unto you, Hereafter ye shall see heaven open, and the angels of God ascending and descending upon the Son of man. JOHN 1:51

14. And this is the Father's will which hath sent me, that of all which he hath given me I should lose nothing, but should raise it up again at the last day. JOHN 6:39

15. The law of the Lord is perfect, converting the soul: the testimony of the Lord is sure, making wise the simple. The statutes of the Lord are

ADVENT KEEPSAKE.

right, rejoicing the heart: the commandment of the Lord is pure, enlightening the eyes. The fear of the Lord is clean, enduring forever: the judgments of the Lord are true and righteous altogether. More to be desired are they than gold, yea, than much fine gold: sweeter also than honey and the honeycomb. Moreover by them is thy servant warned: and in keeping of them there is great reward. PSALM 19:7-11

16. O thou afflicted, tossed with tempest, and not comforted, behold, I will lay thy stones with fair colors, and lay thy foundations with sapphires. And I will make thy windows of agates, and thy gates of carbuncles, and all thy borders of pleasant stones. And all thy children shall be taught of the Lord; and great shall be the peace of thy children. ISAIAH 54:11-13

17. And Jesus answered and said, Verily I say unto you, There is no man that hath left house or brethren, or sisters, or father, or mother, or wife, or children, or lands, for my sake, and the gospel's, but he shall receive an hundred fold now in this time, houses, and brethren, and sisters, and mothers, and children, and lands, with persecutions; and in the world to come eternal life. MARK 10:29-30

JULY.

18. There remaineth therefore a rest to the people of God. HEBREWS 4:9

19. And we desire that every one of you do shew the same diligence to the full assurance of hope unto the end: that ye be not slothful, but followers of them who through faith and patience inherit the promises. HEBREWS 6:11-12

20. Let us therefore fear, lest, a promise being left us of entering into his rest, any of you should seem to come short of it. HEBREWS 4:1

21. But ye, beloved, building up yourselves on your most holy faith, praying in the Holy Ghost, keep yourselves in the love of God, looking for the mercy of our Lord Jesus Christ unto eternal life. JUDE 20,21

22. And have hope toward God, which they themselves also allow, that there shall be a resurrection of the dead, both of the just and unjust. ACTS 24:15

23. Hold thy peace at the presence of the Lord God: for the day of the Lord is at hand: for the Lord hath prepared a sacrifice, he hath bid his guests. And it shall come to pass in the day of the Lord's sacrifice, that I will punish the

ADVENT KEEPSAKE.

princes, and the king's children, and all such as are clothed with strange apparel. ZEPHANIAH 1:7-8

24. And let us consider one another to provoke unto love and to good works: not forsaking the assembling of ourselves together, as the manner of some is; but exhorting one another: and so much the more as ye see the day approaching. HEBREWS 10:24-25

25. How beautiful upon the mountains are the feet of him that bringeth good tidings, that publisheth peace; that bringeth good tidings of good, that publisheth salvation; that saith unto Zion, Thy God reigneth! Thy watchmen shall lift up the voice; with the voice together shall they sing: for they shall see eye to eye, when the Lord shall bring again Zion. ISAIAH 52:7-8

26. For ye have need of patience, that, after ye have done the will of God, ye might receive the promise. HEBREWS 10:36

27. He will swallow up death in victory; and the Lord God will wipe away tears from off all faces; and the rebuke of his people shall he

JULY.

take away from off all the earth; for the Lord hath spoken it. ISAIAH 25:8

28. He which testifieth these things saith, Surely I come quickly; Amen. Even so come, Lord Jesus. REVELATION 22:20

29. The Spirit of the Lord God is upon me; because the Lord hath anointed me to preach good tidings unto the meek; he hath sent me to bind up the brokenhearted, to proclaim liberty to the captives, and the opening of the prison to them that are bound; to proclaim the acceptable year of the Lord, and the day of vengeance of our God; to comfort all that mourn. ISAIAH 61:1-2

30. Wherefore comfort one another with these words. 1 THESSALONIANS 4:18

31. And the Lord make you to increase and abound in love one toward another, and toward all men, even as we do toward you: to the end he may stablish your hearts unblameable in holiness before God, even our Father, at the coming of our Lord Jesus Christ with all his saints. 1 THESSALONIANS 3:12-13

AUGUST.

1. In my Father's house are many mansions: if it were not so, I would have told you. I go to prepare a place for you. And if I go and prepare a place for you, I will come again, and receive you unto myself: that where I am, there ye may be also. JOHN 14:2-3

2. Repent ye therefore, and be converted, that your sins may be blotted out, when the times of refreshing shall come from the presence of the Lord; and he shall send Jesus Christ, which before was preached unto you: whom the Heaven must receive until the times of restitution of all things, which God hath spoken by the mouth of all his holy prophets since the world began. ACTS 3:19-21

3. In that day will I make the governors of Judah like an hearth of fire among the wood, and like a torch of fire in a sheaf; and they shall devour all the people round about, on the right hand and on the left: and Jerusalem shall be inhabited

AUGUST.

again in her own place, even in Jerusalem. ZECHARIAH 12:6

4. The Lord said, I will bring again from Bashan, I will bring my people again from the depths of the sea. PSALM 68:22

5. Then the eyes of the blind shall be opened, and the ears of the deaf shall be unstopped. Then shall the lame man leap as a hart, and the tongue of the dumb sing: for in the wilderness shall waters break out, and streams in the desert. ISAIAH 35:5-6

6. For the earth shall be filled with the knowledge of the glory of the Lord, as the waters cover the sea. HABBAKUK 2:14

7. Thy people also shall be all righteous: they shall inherit the land for ever, the branch of my planting, the work of my hands, that I may be glorified. ISAIAH 60:21

8. Lord, who shall abide in thy tabernacle? who shall dwell in thy holy hill? PSALM 15:1

9. As birds flying, so will the Lord of hosts defend Jerusalem; defending also he will deliver it; and passing over he will preserve it. ISAIAH 31:5

ADVENT KEEPSAKE.

10. Whosoever therefore shall be ashamed of me and of my words in this adulterous and sinful generation; of him also shall the Son of man be ashamed when he cometh in the glory of his Father with the holy angels. MARK 8:88

11. In that day shall the Lord defend the inhabitants of Jerusalem; and he that is feeble among them at that day shall be as David; and the house of David shall be as God, as the angel of the Lord before them. ZECHARIAH 12:8

12. And I will bring the third part through the fire, and will refine them as silver is refined, and will try them as gold is tried: they shall call on my name, and I will hear them: I will say, It is my people: and they shall say, The Lord is my God. ZECHARIAH 13:9

13. Then shall the Lord go forth, and fight against those nations, as when he fought in the day of battle. And his feet shall stand in that day upon the mount of Olives, which is before Jerusalem on the east, and the mount of Olives shall cleave in the midst thereof toward the east and I toward the west, and there shall be a very great valley; and half of the mountain

AUGUST.

shall remove toward the north, and half of it toward the south. ZECHARIAH 14:4

14. But, beloved, remember ye the words which were spoken before of the apostles of our Lord Jesus Christ; how that they told you there should be mockers in the last time, who should walk after their own ungodly lusts. JUDE 17,18

15. Thou wilt shew me the path of j life: in thy presence is fullness of joy; at thy right hand there are pleasures for evermore. PSALM 16:11

16. The righteous shall inherit the land, and dwell therein for ever. PSALM 37:29

17. But the salvation of the righteous is of the Lord: he is their strength in the time of trouble. PSALM 37:39

18. Behold, the righteous shall be recompensed in the earth: much more the wicked and the sinner. PROVERBS 11:31

19. Rejoice greatly, O daughter of Zion; shout, O daughter of Jerusalem: behold, thy King cometh unto thee: he is just, and having salvation; lowly, and riding upon an ass, and upon a colt the foal of an ass. And I will cut off the chariot from Ephraim, and the horse from Jerusalem,

ADVENT KEEPSAKE.

and the battle bow shall be cut off: and he shall speak peace unto the heathen: and his dominion shall be from sea even to sea, and from the river even to the ends of the earth. ZECHARIAH 9:9-10

20. Grudge not one against another, brethren, lest ye be condemned: behold, the Judge standeth before the door. JAMES 5:9

21. And the nations were angry, and thy wrath is come, and the time of the dead, that they should be judged, and that thou shouldest give reward unto thy servants the prophets, and to the saints, and them that fear thy name, small and great; and shouldest destroy them which destroy the earth. REVELATION 11:18

22. The nations shall see and be confounded at all their might: they shall lay their hand upon their mouth, their ears shall be deaf. They shall lick the dust like a serpent, they shall move out of their holes like worms of the earth: they shall be afraid of the Lord our God, and shall fear because of thee. MICAH 7:16

23. But Israel shall be saved in the Lord with an everlasting salvation: ye shall not be ashamed

AUGUST.

nor confounded world without end. ISAIAH 45:17

24. Jesus saith unto her, Thy brother shall rise again. JOHN 11:23

25. For he looked for a city which hath foundations, whose builder and maker is God. HEBREWS 11:10

26. Break forth into joy, sing together, ye waste places of Jerusalem: for the Lord hath comforted his people, he hath redeemed Jerusalem. The Lord hath made bare his holy arm in the eyes of all the nations: and all the ends of the earth shall see the salvation of our God. ISAIAH 52:9-10

27. And this I pray, that your love may abound yet more and more in knowledge and in all judgment; that ye may approve things that are excellent; that ye may be sincere and without offence till the day of Christ. PHILIPPIANS 1:9-10

28. But Jerusalem which is above is free, which is the mother of us all. GALATIANS 4:26

29. And the remnant of Jacob shall be in the midst of many people as a dew from the Lord, as the showers upon the grass, that tarrieth not for

ADVENT KEEPSAKE.

man, nor waiteth for the sons of men. And the remnant of Jacob shall be among the Gentiles in the midst of many people as a lion among the beasts of the forest, as a young lion among the flocks of sheep; who, if he go through, both treadeth down, and teareth in pieces, and none can deliver. MICAH 5:7-8

30. Behold, I have refined thee, but not with silver; I have chosen thee in the furnace of affliction. ISAIAH 48:10

31. Be ye therefore perfect, even as your Father which is in Heaven is perfect. MATTHEW 5:48

SEPTEMBER.

1. For we know that the whole creation groaneth and travaileth in pain together until now. And not only they, but ourselves also, which have the firstfruits of the Spirit, even we ourselves groan within ourselves, waiting for the adoption, to wit, the redemption of our body. ROMANS 8:22-23

2. But of that day and hour knoweth no man, no not the angels of Heaven, but my Father only. MATTHEW 24:36

3. And the times of this ignorance God winked at; but now commandeth all men everywhere to repent: because he hath appointed a day, in the which he will judge the world in righteousness by that man whom he hath ordained; whereof he hath given assurance unto all men, in that he hath raised him from the dead. ACTS 17:30-31

4. But as the days of Xoe were, so shall also the coming of the Son of man be. MATTHEW 24:37

ADVENT KEEPSAKE.

5. Verily I say unto you, This generation shall not pass, till all these things be fulfilled. Heaven and earth shall pass away, but my words shall not pass away. MATTHEW 24:34-35

6. And I will wait upon the Lord, that hideth his face from the house of Jacob, and I will look for him. ISAIAH 8:17

7. For yet a very little while, and the indignation shall cease, and mine anger in their destruction. ISAIAH 10:25

8. And I saw heaven opened, and behold a white horse; and he that sat upon him was called Faithful and True, and in righteousness he doth judge and make war. And he hath on his vesture and on his thigh a name written, KING OF KINGS, AND LORD OF LORDS. REVELATION 19:11,16

9. Behold, I come as a thief. Blessed is he that watcheth, and keepeth his garments, lest he walk naked, and they see his shame. REVELATION 16:15

10. Is it not yet a very little while, and Lebanon shall be turned into a fruitful field, and the fruitful field shall be esteemed as a forest? And

SEPTEMBER.

in that day shall the deaf hear the words of the book, and the eyes of the blind shall see out of obscurity, and out of darkness. ISAIAH 29:17-18

11. And though the Lord give you the bread of adversity, and the water of affliction, yet shall not thy teachers be removed into a corner any more, but thine eyes shall see thy teachers. ISAIAH 30:20

12. And there shall be upon every high mountain, and upon every high hill, rivers and streams of waters in the day of the great slaughter, when the towers fall. Moreover the light of the moon shall be as the light of the sun, and the light of the sun shall be seven-fold, as the light of seven days, in the day that the Lord bindeth up the breach of his people, and healeth the stroke of their wound. ISAIAH 30:25-26

13. And the Lord shall cause his glorious voice to be heard, and shall show the lighting down of his arm, with the indignation of his anger, and with the flame of a devouring fire, with scattering, and tempest, and hailstones. ISAIAH 30:30

ADVENT KEEPSAKE.

14. So shall they fear the name of the Lord from the west, and his glory from the rising of the sun. When the enemy shall come in like a flood, the Spirit of the Lord shall lift up a standard against him. And the Redeemer shall come to Zion, and unto them that turn from transgression in Jacob, saith the Lord. ISAIAH 59:19-20

15. And God hath both raised up the Lord, and will also raise us up by his own power. 1 CORINTHIANS 6:14

16. For as in Adam all die, even so in Christ shall all be made alive. 1 CORINTIANS 15:22

17. And they that shall be of thee shall build the old waste places: thou shalt raise up the foundations of many generations; and thou shalt be called, The repairer of the breach, The restorer of paths to dwell in. If thou turn away thy foot from the Sabbath, from doing thy pleasure on my holy day; and call the Sabbath a delight, the holy of the Lord, honorable; and shalt honor him, not doing thine own ways, nor finding thine own pleasure, nor speaking thine own words: then shalt thou delight thyself in the Lord; and I will cause thee to ride upon the

SEPTEMBER.

high places of the earth, and feed thee with the heritage of Jacob thy father: for the mouth of the Lord hath spoken it. ISAIAH 58:12-14

18. And at that time shall Michael stand up, the great prince which standeth for the children of thy people: and there shall be a time of trouble, such as never was since there was a nation, even to that same time: and at that time thy people shall be delivered, every one that shall be found written in the book. DANIEL 12:1

19. For yourselves know perfectly that the day of the Lord so cometh as a thief in the night. 1 THESSALONIANS 5:2

20. The glory of Lebanon shall come unto thee, the fir tree, the pine tree, and the box together, to beautify the place of my sanctuary; and I will make the place of my feet glorious. The sons also of them that afflicted thee shall come bending unto thee; and all they that despised thee shall bow themselves down at the soles of thy feet; and they shall call thee, The City of the Lord, the Zion of the Holy One of Israel. ISAIAH 60:13-14

21. For as in the days that were before the flood they were eating and drinking, marrying and

ADVENT KEEPSAKE.

giving in marriage, until the day that Noe entered into the ark, and knew not until the flood came, and took them all away; so shall also the coming of the Son of man be. MATTHEW 24:38-39

22. Behold, I shew you a mystery: We shall not all sleep, but we shall all be changed, in a moment, in the twinkling of an eye, at the last trump: for the trumpet shall sound, and the dead shall be raised incorruptible, and we shall be changed. 1 CORINTHIANS 15:51-52

23. For this corruptible must put on, incorruption, and this mortal must put on immortality. So when this corruptible shall have put on incorruption, and this mortal shall have put on immortality, then shall be brought to pass the saying that is written, Death is swallowed up in victory. O death, where is thy sting? O grave, where is thy victory? 1 CORINTHIANS 15:53-55

24. O Lord, be gracious unto us; we have waited for thee: be thou their arm every morning, our salvation also in the time of trouble. ISAIAH 33:2

25. Him that overcometh will I make a pillar in the temple of my God, and he shall go no more

SEPTEMBER.

out: and I will write upon him the name of my God, and the name of the city of my God, which is New Jerusalem, which cometh down out of Heaven from my God: and I will write upon him my new name. REVELATION 3:12

26. We know that, if our earthly house of this tabernacle were dissolved, we have a building of God, a house not made with hands, eternal in the Heavens. For in this we groan, earnestly desiring to be clothed upon with our house which is from Heaven: if so be that being clothed we shall not be found naked. For we that are in this tabernacle do groan, being burdened: not for that we would be unclothed, but clothed upon, that mortality might be swallowed up of life. 2 CORINTHIANS 5:1-4

27. Behold, the days come, saith the Lord, that the ploughman shall overtake the reaper, and the treader of grapes him that soweth seed: and the mountains shall drop sweet wine, and all the hills shall melt. And I will bring again the captivity of my people of Israel, and they shall build the waste cities, and inhabit them; and they shall plant vineyards, and drink the wine thereof; they shall also make gardens, and eat the fruit of them. And I will plant them upon

ADVENT KEEPSAKE.

their land, and they shall no more be pulled up out of their land which I have given them, saith the Lord thy God. AMOS 9:13-15

28. The wolf also shall dwell with the lamb, and the leopard shall lie down with the kid; and the calf and the young lion and the fatling together; and a little child shall lead them. And the cow and the bear shall feed; their young ones shall lie down together: and the lion shall eat straw like the ox. And the sucking child shall play on the hole of the asp, and the weaned child shall put his hand on the cockatrice's den. They shall not hurt nor destroy in all my holy mountain: for the earth shall be full of the knowledge of the Lord, as the waters cover the sea. ISAIAH 11:6-9

29. And the work of righteousness shall be peace; and the effect of righteousness quietness and assurance forever. And my people shall dwell in a peaceable habitation, and in sure dwellings, and in quiet resting places. ISAIAH 32:17-18

30. And in this mountain shall the Lord of hosts make unto all people a feast of fat things, a feast of wines on the lees, of fat things full of marrow, of wines on the lees well refined. And

SEPTEMBER.

he will destroy in this mountain the face of the covering cast over all people, and the vail that is spread over all nations. ISAIAH 25:6-7

OCTOBER.

1. Behold, I stand at the door, and knock: If any man hear my voice, and open the door, I will come in to him, and will sup with him, and he with me. REVELATION 3:20

2. To him that overcometh will I grant to sit with me in my throne, even as I also overcame, and am set down with my Father in his throne. REVELATION 3:21

3. He that dwelleth in the secret place of the Most High shall abide under the shadow of the Almighty. I will say of the Lord, He is my refuge and my fortress: my God; in him will I trust. Surely he shall deliver thee from the snare of the fowler, and from the noisome pestilence. He shall cover thee with his feathers, and under his wings shalt thou trust: his truth shall be thy shield and buckler. PSALM 91:1-4

4. Because he hath set his love upon me, therefore will I deliver him: I will set him on high, because he hath known my name. He shall call upon

OCTOBER.

me, and I will answer him: I will be with him in trouble; I will deliver him, and honor him. With long life will I satisfy him, and shew him my salvation. PSALM 91:14-16

5. Thy dead men shall live, together with my dead body shall they arise. Awake and sing, ye that dwell in dust: for thy dew is as the dew of herbs, and the earth shall cast out the dead. ISAIAH 26:19

6. Come, my people, enter thou into thy chambers, and shut thy doors about thee: hide thyself as it were for a little moment, until the indignation be over-past. ISAIAH 26:20

7. Howl ye; for the day of the Lord is at hand; it shall come as a destruction from the Almighty. Therefore shall all hands be faint, and every man's heart shall melt. ISAIAH 13:6-7

8. I will make a man more precious than fine gold; even a man than the golden wedge of Ophir. Therefore I will shake the heavens, and the earth shall remove out of her place, in the wrath of the Lord of hosts, and in the day of his fierce anger. ISAIAH 13:12-13

ADVENT KEEPSAKE.

9. Woe to the multitude of many people, which make a noise like the noise of the seas; and to the rushing of nations, that make a rushing like the rushing of mighty waters! The nations shall rush like the rushing of many waters: but God shall rebuke them, and they shall flee far off, and shall be chased as the chaff of the mountains before the wind, and like a rolling thing before the whirlwind. And behold at eveningtide trouble; and before the morning he is not. This is the portion of them that spoil us, and the lot of them that rob us. ISAIAH 17:12-14

10. The burden of Dumah. He calleth to me out of Seir, Watchman, what of the night? Watchman, what of the night? The watchman said, The morning cometh, and also the night: if ye will inquire, inquire ye: return, come. ISAIAH 11:11-12

11. Behold, the Lord maketh the earth empty, and maketh it waste, and turneth it upside down, and scattereth abroad the inhabitants thereof. And it shall be, as with the people, so with the priest; as with the servant, so with his master; as with the maid, so with her mistress; as with the buyer, so with the seller; as with

OCTOBER.

the lender, so with the borrower; as with the taker of usury, so with the giver of usury to him. The land shall be utterly emptied, and utterly spoiled: for the Lord hath spoken this word. ISAIAH 14:1-3

12. The earth shall reel to and fro like a drunkard, and shall be removed like a cottage; and the transgression thereof shall be heavy upon it; and it shall fall, and not rise again. ISAIAH 24:20

13. And it shall be said in that day, Lo, this is our God; we have waited for him, and he will save us: this is the Lord; we have waited for him, we will be glad and rejoice in his salvation. ISAIAH 25:9

14. In that day shall this song be sung in the land of Judah: We have a strong city; salvation will God appoint for walls and bulwarks. Open ye the gates, that the righteous nation which keepeth the truth may enter in. ISAIAH 26:1-2

15. Think not that I am come to destroy the law or the prophets: I am not I come to destroy, but to fulfill. For verily I say unto you, Till heaven and earth pass, one jot or one tittle

ADVENT KEEPSAKE.

shall in no wise pass from the law, till all be fulfilled. MATTHEW 5:17-18

16. But evil men and seducers shall wax worse and worse, deceiving and being deceived. 2 TIMOTHY 3:13

17. But they that wait upon the Lord shall renew their strength; they shall mount up with wings as eagles; they shall run, and not be weary; and they shall walk, and not faint. ISAIAH 40:31

18. The Lord thy God in the midst of thee is mighty; he will save, he will rejoice over thee with joy; he will rest in his love, he will joy over thee with singing. I will gather them that are sorrowful for the solemn assembly, who are of thee, to whom the reproach of it was a burden. HABBAKUK 3:17-18

19. The Lord shall go forth as a mighty man, he shall stir up jealousy like a man. For ye shall go out with joy, and be led forth with peace: the mountains and the hills shall break forth before you into singing, and all the trees of the field shall clap their hands. Instead of the thorn shall come up the fir tree, and instead of the brier shall come up the myrtle tree: and it shall be to the Lord for a name, for

OCTOBER.

an everlasting sign that shall not be cut off. ISAIAH 55:12-13

20. And I will bring the blind by a way that they knew not: I will lead them in paths that they have not known: I will make darkness light before them, and crooked things straight. These things will I do unto them, and not forsake them. ISAIAH 42:16

21. Thine eyes shall see the King in his beauty: they shall behold the land that is very far off. ISAIAH 33:17

22. I have blotted out, as a thick cloud thy transgressions, and, as a cloud, thy sins: return unto me; for I have redeemed thee. Sing, O ye heavens; for the Lord hath done it: shout, ye lower parts of the earth: break forth into singing, ye mountains, O forest, and every tree therein: for the Lord hath redeemed Jacob, and glorified himself in Israel. ISAIAH 44:22-23

23. And I saw another angel fly in the midst of heaven, having the everlasting gospel to preach unto them that dwell on the earth, and to every nation, and kindred, and tongue, and people, saying with a loud voice, Fear God and give glory to him, for the hour of his judgment is

ADVENT KEEPSAKE.

come: and worship him that made heaven, and earth, and the sea, and the fountains of waters. REVELATION 14:6-7

24. When thou passest through the waters, I will be with thee; and through the rivers, they shall not overflow thee: when thou walkest through the fire, thou shalt not be burned; neither shall the flame kindle upon thee. ISAIAH 43:2

25. God, who at sundry times and in divers manners spake in time past unto the fathers by the prophets, hath in these last days spoken unto us by his Son. HEBREWS 1:1-2

26. Remember therefore how thou hast received and heard, and hold fast and repent. If therefore thou shalt not watch, I will come on thee as a thief, and thou shalt not know what hour I will come upon thee. REVELATION 3:3

27. Make the heart of this people fat, and make their ears heavy, and shut their eyes; lest they see with their eyes, and hear with their ears, and understand with their heart, and convert, and be healed. Then said I, Lord, how long? And he answered, Until the cities be wasted without inhabitant, and the houses without man, and the land be utterly desolate, and the

OCTOBER.

Lord have removed men far away, and there be a great forsaking in the midst of the land. ISAIAH 6:10-12

28. But blessed are your eyes, for they see: and your ears, for they hear. MATTHEW 13:6

29. Be ye also patient; stablish your hearts: for the coming of the Lord draweth nigh. JAMES 5:8

30. But that which ye have already, hold fast till I come. REVELATION 2:25

31. The Son of man shall send forth his angels, and they shall gather out of his kingdom all things that offend, and them which do iniquity; and shall cast them into a furnace of fire: there shall be wailing and gnashing of teeth. Then shall the righteous shine forth as the sun in the kingdom of their Father. MATTHEW 13:41-43

NOVEMBER.

1. Blessed be the God and Father of our Lord Jesus Christ, which according to his abundant mercy hath begotten us again unto a lively hope, by the resurrection of Jesus Christ from the dead, to an inheritance incorruptible, and undefiled, and that fadeth not away, reserved in Heaven for you, who are kept by the power of God through faith unto salvation ready to be revealed in the last time. 1 PETER 1:3-5

2. In my distress I called upon the Lord, and cried unto my God: he heard my voice out of his temple, and my cry came before him, even into his ears. Then the earth shook and trembled; the found- ations also of the hills moved and were shaken, because he was wroth. There went up a smoke out of his nostrils, and fire out of his mouth devoured: coals were kindled by it. He bowed the heavens also, and came down: and darkness was under his feet. PSALM 18:6-9

NOVEMBER.

3. The Lord shall roar from on high, and utter his voice from his holy habitation; he shall mightily roar upon his habitation; he shall give a shout, as they that tread the grapes, against all the inhabit- ants of the earth. JEREMIAH 25:30

4. And He rode upon a cherub, and did fly: yea, he did fly upon the wings of the wind. He made darkness his secret place; his pavilion round about him were dark waters and thick clouds of the skies. At the brightness that was before him his thick clouds passed, hailstones and coals of fire. PSALM 18:10-12

5. The Lord also thundered in the heavens, and the Highest gave his voice; hailstones and coals of fire. Yea, he sent out his arrows, and scattered them; and he shot out lightnings, and discomfited them. Then the channels of waters were seen, and the foundations of the world were discovered at thy rebuke, O Lord, at the blast of the breath of thy nostrils. He sent from above, he took me, he drew me out of many waters. PSALM 18:13-16

6. He delivered me from my strong enemy, and from them which hated me: for they were too strong for me. They prevented me in the day

ADVENT KEEPSAKE.

of my calamity: but the Lord was my stay. He brought me forth also into a large place; he delivered me, because he delighted in me. PSALM 18:17-19

7. The Lord rewarded me according to my righteousness; according to the cleanness of my hands hath he recompensed me. For I have kept the ways of the Lord, and have not wickedly departed from my God. For all his judgments were before me, and I did not put away his statutes from me. PSALM 18:20-22

8. The Lord also shall roar out of Zion, and utter his voice from Jerusalem; and the heavens and the earth shall shake: but the Lord will be the hope of his people, and the strength of the children of Israel. JOEL 3:16

9. But the heavens and the earth, which are now, by the same word are kept in store, reserved unto fire against the day of judgment and perdition of ungodly men. 2 PETER 3:7

10. Lift up your eyes to the heavens, and look upon the earth beneath: for the heavens shall vanish away like smoke, and the earth shall wax old like a garment, and they that dwell therein shall die in like manner: but my salvation shall

NOVEMBER.

be forever, if and my righteousness shall not be abolished. ISAIAH 51:6

11. Therefore the redeemed of the Lord shall return, and come with singing unto Zion; and everlasting joy shall be upon their head: they shall obtain gladness and joy; and sorrow and mourning shall flee away. ISAIAH 51:11

12. They shall not hunger nor thirst; neither shall the heat nor sun smite them: for He that hath mercy on them shall lead them, even by the springs of water shall he guide them. ISAIAH 49:10

13. For whosoever will save his life shall lose.it: and whosoever will lose his life for my sake shall find it. MATTHEW 16:25

14. For the Lord shall comfort Zion: he will comfort her waste places; and he will make her wilderness like Eden, and her desert like the garden of the Lord, joy and gladness shall be found therein; thanksgiving, and the voice of melody. ISAIAH 51:9

15. He shall dwell on high: his place of defense shall be the munitions of rocks: bread shall

ADVENT KEEPSAKE.

be given him; his waters shall be sure. ISAIAH 33:16

16. Wherefore gird up the loins of your mind, be sober, and hope to the end for the grace that is to be brought unto you at the revelation of Jesus Christ. 1 PETER 1:13

17. And that, knowing the time, that now it is high time to awake out of sleep: for now is our salvation nearer than when 1 we believed. ROMANS 13:11

18. If by any means I might attain unto the resurrection of the dead. PHILIPPIANS 3:11

19. Looking for that blessed hope, and the glorious appearing of the great God and our Saviour Jesus Christ. TITUS 2:13

20. And to wait for his Son from Heaven, whom he raised from the dead, even if Jesus, which delivered us trom the wrath to come. 1 THESSALONIANS 1:10

21. And I will make her that halted a remnant, and her that was cast far off a strong nation: and the Lord shall reign over them in Mount Zion from henceforth, even forever. And thou, 0 Tower of the flock, the strong hold of the

NOVEMBER.

daughter of Zion, unto thee shall it come, even the first dominion; the kingdom shall come to the daughter of Jerusalem. MICAH 4:7-8

22. But in the days of the voice of the seventh angel, when he shall begin to sound, the mystery of God should be finished, as he hath declared to his servants the prophets. REVELATION 10:7

23. There shall come in the last days scoffers, walking after their own lusts, and saying, Where is the promise of His coming? for since the fathers fell asleep, all things continue as they were from the beginning of the creation. 2 PETER 3:3-4

24. Who shall give account to Him that is ready to judge the quick and the dead. 1 PETER 4:5

25. Know ye not that we shall judge angels? 1 CORINTIANS 6:3

26. Thy kingdom come. MATTHEW 6:9

27. Repent ye; for the kingdom of heaven is at hand. MATHEW 3:1

28. But when they persecute you in this city, flee ye into another: for verily I say unto you, Ye

ADVENT KEEPSAKE.

shall not have gone over the cities of Israel, till the Son of man be come. MATTHEW 10:23

29. And as ye go, preach, saying, The kingdom of heaven is at hand. MATTHEW 10:7

30. But I say unto you, I will not drink henceforth of this fruit of the vine, until that day when I drink it new with you in my Father's kingdom. MATTHEW 26:29

DECEMBER.

1. Blow ye the trumpet in Zion, and sound an alarm in my holy mountain: let all the inhabitants of the land tremble; for the day of the Lord cometh, for it is nigh at hand. JOEL 2:1

2. And it shall come to pass, that whosoever shall call on the name of the Lord shall be delivered: for in mount Zion and in Jerusalem shall be deliverance, as the Lord hath said, and in the remnant whom the Lord shall call. JOEL 2:33

3. For the Lord himself shall descend from Heaven with a shout, with the voice of the archangel, and with the trump of God: and the dead in Christ shall rise first. 1 THESSALONIANS 4:16

4. But ye, brethren, are not in darkness, that that day should overtake you as a thief. 1 THESSALONIANS 5:4

5. Behold, the days come, saith the Lord, that I will raise unto David a righteous Branch, and a King shall reign and prosper, and shall execute

ADVENT KEEPSAKE.

judgment and justice in the earth. In his days Judah shall be saved, and Israel shall dwell safely: and this is his name whereby he shall be called, THE LORD OUR RIGHTEOUSNESS. JEREMIAH 23:5-6

6. And I will make with them a covenant of peace, and will cause the evil beasts to cease out of the land; and they shall dwell safely in the wilderness, and sleep in the woods. EZEKIEL 34:25

7. Receiving the end of your faith, even the salvation of your souls. 1 PETER 1:9

8. Behold, O my people, I will open your graves, and cause you to come up out of your graves, and bring you into the land of Israel. And ye shall know that I am the Lord, when I have opened your graves, O my people, and brought you up out of your graves, and shall put my Spirit in you, and ye shall live, and I shall place you in your own land: then shall ye know that I the Lord have spoken it, and performed it, saith the Lord. EZEKIEL 37:12-14

9. For, behold, I create new heavens and a new earth, and the former shall not be remembered, nor come into mind. ISAIAH 65:17

DECEMBER.

10. And they shall build houses, and inhabit them; and they shall plant vineyards, and eat the fruit of them. They shall not build, and another inhabit; they shall not plant, and another eat: for as the days of a tree are the days of my people and mine elect shall long enjoy the work of their hands. ISAIAH 65:21-22

11. For as the new heavens and the new earth, which I will make, shall remain before me, saith the Lord, so shall your seed and your name remain. ISAIAH 66:22

12. But the Lord is the true God, he is the living God, and an everlasting King: at his wrath the earth shall tremble, and the nations shall not be able to abide his indignation. JEREMIAH 10:10

13. Alas! for that day is great, so that none is like it: it is even the time of Jacob's trouble; but he shall be saved out of it. JEREMIAH 30:7

14. That the trial of your faith, being much more precious than of gold that perisheth, though it be tried with fire, might be found unto praise and honor and glory at the appearing of Jesus Christ. 1 PETER 1:1

ADVENT KEEPSAKE.

15. Thus saith the Lord God, Remove the diadem, and take off the crown: this shall not be the same: exalt him that is low, and abase him that is high. I will overturn, overturn, overturn it: and it shall be no more, until He come whose right it is; and I will give it him. EZEKIEL 21:26-27

16. And in the days of these kings shall the God of Heaven set up a kingdom, which shall never be destroyed: and the kingdom shall not be left to other people, but it shall break in pieces and consume all these kingdoms, and it shall stand forever. DAMIEL 2:44

17. For what is our hope, or joy, or crown of rejoicing? Are not even ye in the presence of our Lord Jesus Christ at his coming? 1 THESSALONIANS 2:19

18. But Christ as a son over his own house; whose house are we, if we hold fast the confidence and the rejoicing of the hope firm unto the end. HEBREWS 3:6

19. Being confident of this very thing, that he which hath begun a good work in you will perform it until the day of Jesus Christ. PHILIPPIANS 1:6

DECEMBER.

20. Let your moderation be known unto all men. The Lord is at hand. PHILIPPIANS 4:5

21. If a man die, shall he live again? All the days of my appointed time will I wait, till my change come. JOB 14:14

22. But I would not have you to be ignorant, brethren, concerning them which are asleep, that ye sorrow not, even as others which hare no hope. For if we believe that Jesus died and rose again, even so them also which sleep in Jesus will God bring with him. 1 THESSALONIANS 4:13-14

23. For this we say unto you by the word of the Lord, that we which are alive and remain unto the coming of the Lord shall not prevent them which are asleep. 1 THESSALONIANS 4:15

24. Then we which are alive and remain shall be caught up together with them in the clouds, to meet the Lord in the air: and so shall we ever be with the Lord. 1 THESSALONIANS 4:17

25. I thank my God always on your behalf, for the grace of God which is given you by Jesus Christ; that in every thing ye are enriched by him, in all utterance, and in all knowledge; even as

ADVENT KEEPSAKE.

the testimony of Christ was confirmed in you: so that ye come behind in no gift; waiting for the coming of our Lord Jesus Christ: who shall also confirm you unto the end, that ye may be blameless in the day of our Lord Jesus Christ. 1 CORINTHIANS 1:4-8

26. Sanctify ye a fast, call a solemn assembly, gather the elders and all the inhabitants of the land into the house of the Lord your God, and cry unto the Lord, Alas for the day! for the day of the Lord is at hand, and as a destruction from the Almighty shall it come. JOEL 1:14-15

27. I beheld till the thrones were cast down, and the Ancient of days did sit, whose garment was white as snow, and the hair of his head like the pure wool: his throne was like the fiery flame, and his wheels as burning fire. A fiery stream issued and came forth from before him: thousand thousands ministered unto him, and ten thousand times ten thousand stood before him: the Judgment was set, and the books were opened. DANIEL 7:9-10

28. I saw in the night visions, and, behold, one like the Son of man came with the clouds of heaven, and came to the Ancient of days,

DECEMBER.

and they brought him near before him. And there was given him dominion, and glory, and a kingdom, that all people, nations, and languages, should serve him: his dominion is an everlasting dominion, which shall not pass away, and his kingdom that which shall not be destroyed. DANIEL 7:13-14

29. And many of them that sleep in the dust of the earth shall awake, some to everlasting life, and some to shame and everlasting contempt. And they that be wise shall shine as the brightness of the firmament; and they that turn many to righteousness, as the stars for ever and ever. DANIEL 12:2-3

30. And it shall come to pass in that day, that the mountains shall drop down new wine, and the hills shall flow with milk, and all the rivers of Judah shall flow with waters, and a fountain shall come forth of the house of the Lord, and shall water the valley of Shittim. JOEL 3:18

31. Now the God of peace, that brought again from the dead our Lord Jesus, that great Shepherd of the sheep, through the blood of the everlasting covenant, make you perfect in every good work to do his will, working in you that which is well pleasing in his sight, through Jesus Christ;

ADVENT KEEPSAKE.

to whom be glory for ever and ever. Amen.
HEBREWS 13:20-21

www.ingramcontent.com/pod-product-compliance
Lightning Source LLC
Chambersburg PA
CBHW050040080526
44586CB00014B/1381